THE ART OF

A Comprehensive Guide to the techniques and patterns in Japanese Arts

KENZO HIROSHI
Copyright@2024

Table of Contents

Chapter 1

    Kumihimo

    Applications of Kumihimo

    Types of Kumihimo

    History of Kumihimo

    Kumihimo tools and materials

    Workspace Needed

Chapter 2

    Fundamental Techniques

    INTERMEDIATE TECHNIQUES

    ADVANCED TECHNIQUES

    Troubleshooting and solutions

Chapter 3

    BEGINNERS PROJECT

    INTERMEDIATE PROJECTS

    ADVANCED PROJECTS

    TIPS FOR SUCCESS

    Conclusion

Chapter 1

Kumihimo

Kumihimo is a traditional Japanese art form involving the creation of intricate braided cords. The name "kumihimo" translates to "gathered threads," indicative of the process by which multiple strands are interwoven to form strong, decorative braids. This technique has been a significant part of Japanese culture for centuries, serving both functional and aesthetic purposes.

Applications of Kumihimo

Kumihimo braids are used in a wide variety of applications:

- **Jewelry**: Bracelets, necklaces, and earrings are popular items, often enhanced with beads and charms.
- **Fashion Accessories**: Belts, laces, and trims for garments, providing both functionality and aesthetic appeal.
- **Home Decor**: Decorative cords for items like curtains, pillows, and other household textiles.
- **Functional Uses**: Utility cords for items such as drawstrings, bag handles, and shoelaces.

Modern Kumihimo

Today, kumihimo continues to be a cherished craft both in Japan and globally. It has experienced a revival due to its meditative quality and the beauty of the resulting braids. Modern enthusiasts can learn kumihimo through:

- **Workshops and Classes**: Offering hands-on experience with guidance from skilled instructors.

- **Online Resources**: Tutorials, videos, and forums provide accessible learning opportunities.
- **Community Groups**: Local and online communities where crafters can share techniques, patterns, and projects.

Kumihimo is a versatile and ancient Japanese braiding art that combines functionality and beauty. Its rich history, coupled with its intricate techniques and varied applications, makes it a unique and rewarding craft for both traditional and contemporary artisans.

Types of Kumihimo

Kumihimo encompasses a variety of braiding techniques, each creating distinct patterns and textures. Here are some of the most common types of kumihimo braids:

1. Kongo Gumi (Basic Round Braid)

- **Description**: The most common kumihimo braid, characterized by its round shape. Typically involves 8 to 16 strands.

- **Applications**: Used for jewelry, laces, and decorative cords.

2. Edo Yatsu Gumi (Square Braid)

- **Description**: A flat, square-shaped braid made with 8 strands. Known for its sturdiness and consistent texture.
- **Applications**: Ideal for belts, straps, and decorative edges on garments.

3. Kara Uchi Gumi (Hollow Braid)

- **Description**: A tubular braid with a hollow center, often created using 12 or more strands.
- **Applications**: Suitable for necklaces, thicker cords, and ornamental purposes.

4. Hira Kara Gumi (Flat Braid)

- **Description**: A flat braid with a lace-like appearance, created using multiple strands. The number of strands can vary, resulting in different widths and patterns.
- **Applications**: Used for obi (sashes), decorative trims, and intricate jewelry.

5. Yatsu Sen (Complex Interlaced Braid)

- **Description**: An advanced braid that involves interlacing multiple strands to create intricate and detailed patterns.
- **Applications**: Ideal for elaborate jewelry pieces, decorative cords, and artistic projects.

6. Ayatake Gumi (Braided Diamond)

- **Description**: A braid featuring a diamond pattern, achieved by manipulating multiple strands in a specific sequence.
- **Applications**: Suitable for decorative purposes and detailed designs on various items.

7. Nami Kawa Gumi (Wave Pattern Braid)

- **Description**: This braid mimics the appearance of waves, created by alternating the movement of the strands.
- **Applications**: Used for decorative cords, jewelry, and textile embellishments.

8. Beaded Kumihimo

- **Description**: Incorporates beads into the braiding process, adding texture and visual interest to the braid.

- **Applications**: Popular in jewelry making, especially for bracelets and necklaces. The beads can be added in various patterns to enhance the visual appeal of the braid.

9. Zaguri Gumi (Spiral Braid)

- **Description**: A braid with a spiral pattern, achieved by rotating the strands around the core in a specific manner.
- **Applications**: Suitable for decorative cords, jewelry, and artistic projects, giving a dynamic, swirling appearance.

10. Kagome Gumi (Basket Weave Braid)

- **Description**: This braid mimics a basket weave pattern, creating a flat, interwoven look. It typically uses a higher number of strands to achieve the intricate design.

- **Applications**: Used for decorative items, belts, and trims that require a detailed, woven appearance.

11. Taka Dai Gumi (Flat Braiding on a Taka Dai Loom)

- **Description**: A flat braid created using a taka dai loom, allowing for wide and complex patterns. The loom supports multiple strands and complex movements.
- **Applications**: Ideal for wide belts, sashes, and other flat decorative pieces.

12. Ajiro Gumi (Fishnet Braid)

- **Description**: Resembling a fishnet, this braid involves creating a network of interconnected loops. It is an open, airy braid often used in decorative applications.
- **Applications**: Suitable for creating light, decorative cords and accessories with an intricate, net-like structure.

History of Kumihimo

Kumihimo has a rich history that spans over a millennium, deeply rooted in Japanese culture and tradition.

Ancient Origins

- **Nara Period (710-794 AD)**: The earliest known use of kumihimo can be traced back to this period. Initially, it was used for religious and ceremonial purposes. Monks and priests used kumihimo cords in temples and shrines.
- **Heian Period (794-1185 AD)**: Kumihimo gained prominence among the aristocracy. The intricate braids were used in court attire and for tying ceremonial objects. This period saw the development of more complex patterns and techniques.
- **Samurai Era**: Samurai warriors adopted kumihimo to lace their armor (known as "odoshi"). The braids not only provided strength and functionality but also served as a status symbol, with elaborate designs indicating higher rank.

Edo Period (1603-1868 AD)

- During the Edo period, kumihimo techniques flourished and became more refined. The demand for kumihimo braids increased, especially in the fashion of the time. Braids were used in traditional Japanese garments like kimonos, particularly in the form of obijime (decorative cords for securing obi sashes). This era also saw the development of specific tools like the marudai and takadai, which allowed for more intricate braiding techniques.

Meiji Period (1868-1912 AD) to Modern Times

- With the modernization of Japan during the Meiji period, the traditional art of kumihimo faced decline. However, it experienced a revival in the 20th century as part of a broader interest in preserving traditional crafts. Today, kumihimo is celebrated both as a traditional art form and a contemporary craft, with artisans and hobbyists exploring its techniques worldwide.

Kumihimo tools and materials

Kumihimo braiding requires a variety of specialized tools and materials. These tools help achieve the precision and intricacy characteristic of traditional and contemporary kumihimo braids.

Tools

1. Marudai

- **Description**: A traditional wooden braiding stand with a round top, supported by four legs.
- **Use**: Threads are draped over the top and weighted with tama (bobbins) to maintain tension. The marudai allows for even, consistent braiding, making it ideal for complex patterns.

- **Features**: The marudai typically has an opening in the center and can accommodate a large number of threads, making it suitable for creating both simple and intricate braids.

2. Disk and Plate

- **Description**: Modern, portable alternatives to the marudai, typically made of foam or plastic. Disks are round, while plates are square.
- **Use**: These tools are used to create braids on the go and are especially popular among beginners and hobbyists. Threads are slotted into numbered notches around the edge to keep them organized.
- **Features**: Lightweight and easy to handle, these tools are convenient for travel and smaller projects.

3. Tama (Bobbins)

- **Description**: Small spools used to manage and control the threads.
- **Use**: They prevent tangling and ensure even tension throughout the braiding process. Tama can be weighted to help maintain consistent thread tension.

- **Features**: Tama come in various sizes and weights, allowing for customization depending on the thickness and length of the threads being used.

4. Kakudai

- **Description**: A square braiding stand used for creating flat braids.
- **Use**: Similar to the marudai but with a square top, making it suitable for specific types of braids.
- **Features**: Helps in maintaining the structure and tension required for flat braids.

5. Takadai

- **Description**: A braiding loom used for more complex braids.
- **Use**: Allows for the creation of intricate patterns and wider braids. The takadai supports multiple strands and complex movements.
- **Features**: Typically used for advanced braiding techniques, offering more versatility in design.

Materials

1. Silk

- **Description**: Traditionally used material known for its smooth texture and vibrant colors.
- **Use**: Provides a luxurious finish and is ideal for high-quality, decorative braids.
- **Features**: Durable, with a natural sheen that enhances the appearance of the braid.

2. Cotton

- **Description**: A versatile and durable material.
- **Use**: Suitable for everyday items and practical applications.
- **Features**: Available in various colors and thicknesses, easy to work with, and comfortable to wear.

3. Nylon

- **Description**: A strong and resilient synthetic material.
- **Use**: Commonly used for jewelry making due to its durability and flexibility.

- **Features**: Available in a wide range of colors, often used with beads and other decorative elements.

4. Polyester

- **Description**: Another synthetic material, similar to nylon but often softer.
- **Use**: Used for both practical and decorative braids.
- **Features**: Durable, resistant to wear and tear, and available in many colors.

5. Metallic Threads

- **Description**: Threads made from metal or with a metallic finish.
- **Use**: Add a decorative, shiny element to braids, making them suitable for special occasions and ornamental purposes.
- **Features**: Often combined with other materials to create striking patterns.

6. Leather

- **Description**: Strips of leather used as threads.

- **Use**: Provides a unique texture and strength, ideal for rustic and robust designs.
- **Features**: Adds a tactile and visual richness to the braid.

7. Wire

- **Description**: Thin, flexible wire.
- **Use**: Used for creating structured, durable braids, often in jewelry making.
- **Features**: Can be shaped and molded, maintaining the structure of the braid.

8. Beads and Charms

- **Description**: Decorative elements added to the threads.
- **Use**: Enhance the visual appeal of the braid, often used in jewelry and decorative items.
- **Features**: Available in various shapes, sizes, and materials, allowing for endless customization.

Workspace Needed

Creating kumihimo braids requires a dedicated workspace that accommodates the tools and materials essential for this intricate craft. Here's a guide to setting up your kumihimo workspace:

1. Surface Area

- **Table or Desk**: Choose a sturdy, flat surface large enough to accommodate your braiding tools and materials. A table or desk of sufficient size ensures stability and comfort during braiding sessions.

2. Braiding Tools

- **Marudai or Disk/Plate**: Depending on your preference and space available, set up either a traditional marudai or a modern disk/plate braiding tool. Ensure it is positioned at a comfortable height for sitting and braiding.
- **Tama (Bobbins)**: Arrange your tama in an accessible manner. They should be within reach to easily manage and swap out threads during braiding.

3. Storage and Organization

- **Bobbins and Threads**: Use containers or organizers to keep your bobbins and threads neatly arranged and easily accessible. This helps prevent tangling and ensures smooth braiding sessions.
- **Tools and Accessories**: Store additional tools such as scissors, rulers, and bead containers nearby for convenience.

4. Lighting

- **Task Lighting**: Ensure adequate lighting directed towards your workspace. Good lighting is essential for working with fine threads and intricate patterns, reducing eye strain and enhancing accuracy.

5. Comfort and Ergonomics

- **Seating**: Choose a comfortable chair with good back support to maintain posture during long braiding sessions.
- **Reach and Accessibility**: Arrange your tools and materials within arm's reach to minimize movement and maximize efficiency while braiding.

6. Ventilation

- **Airflow**: Ensure your workspace has adequate ventilation, especially if working with adhesives or finishes. Good airflow helps maintain comfort and safety during crafting.

7. Safety

- **Tool Safety**: Keep sharp tools and materials out of reach of children and pets. Use caution when handling scissors, blades, or other sharp objects.

8. Inspiration and Creativity

- **Decor and Inspiration**: Personalize your workspace with items that inspire creativity, such as photos, artwork, or samples of completed kumihimo projects.

9. Cleaning and Maintenance

- **Maintenance Tools**: Keep cleaning supplies handy for maintaining your braiding tools and workspace. This ensures they remain in good condition for continued use.

10. Flexibility and Adaptability

- **Adjustable Setup**: Consider the flexibility of your workspace setup. Adjustable height tables or ergonomic accessories can enhance comfort and accommodate different braiding techniques.

By organizing your workspace effectively and ensuring it meets your ergonomic needs, you can create an environment conducive to enjoyable and productive kumihimo braiding sessions. Whether you prefer traditional techniques or modern tools, a well-equipped workspace enhances creativity and craftsmanship in this ancient Japanese art form.

Chapter 2

Fundamental Techniques

Creating kumihimo involves mastering fundamental braiding techniques that form the basis for various patterns and designs. Here are step-by-step instructions for three fundamental kumihimo techniques using a round disk, suitable for beginners:

Materials Needed:

- Kumihimo disk (round)
- Scissors
- Tama (bobbins) with thread (different colors for contrast)
- Optional: Weighted bobbins or clips to maintain tension

1. **Kongo Gumi (Basic Round Braid)**

Step 1: Prepare Your Materials

1. **Thread Setup**: Cut four strands of thread, each approximately 1.5 meters (5 feet) long.
2. **Load Bobbins**: Thread each strand through a bobbin and secure the ends by winding them around the slots on the disk.

Step 2: Set Up the Kumihimo Disk

1. **Arrange Threads**: Place the threads into the slots of the kumihimo disk according to the desired pattern (for a basic round braid, place one color in each slot).
2. **Positioning**: Place the disk flat on your workspace with the dot at the top.

Step 3: Braiding Process

1. **Start Braiding**: Rotate the disk so the empty slot is at the top (12 o'clock position).
2. **Move the Threads**: Take the bottom thread from the slot to the right of the empty slot (move it counter-clockwise) and move it into the empty slot.

3. **Turn the Disk**: Rotate the disk so the next empty slot is at the top.
4. **Repeat**: Continue moving the bottom thread into the empty slot, rotating the disk after each move. Maintain even tension on the threads as you braid.

Step 4: Finishing

1. **Continue Braiding**: Repeat the braiding process until the braid reaches the desired length.
2. **Secure the End**: Once finished, remove the threads from the disk and secure the ends with a temporary knot or clip to prevent unraveling.

2. Edo Yatsu Gumi (Square Braid)

Step 1: Prepare Your Materials

1. **Thread Setup**: Cut eight strands of thread, each approximately 1 meter (3 feet) long.
2. **Load Bobbins**: Thread each strand through a bobbin and secure them on the kumihimo disk.

Step 2: Set Up the Kumihimo Disk

1. **Arrange Threads**: Insert the threads into the slots of the kumihimo disk. Arrange them so that each pair of opposite slots has threads of the same color.
2. **Positioning**: Place the disk flat on your workspace with the dot at the top.

Step 3: Braiding Process

1. **Start Braiding**: Begin by taking the bottom-left thread and move it to the top-left slot.
2. **Turn the Disk**: Rotate the disk so the bottom-right thread is now at the top-right slot.

3. **Continue Braiding**: Repeat the process, moving the bottom threads to the top slots in a diagonal pattern (left to right, then right to left).
4. **Maintain Tension**: Keep the tension even as you rotate the disk and move the threads.

Step 4: Finishing

1. **Repeat Braiding**: Continue braiding until the desired length is reached.
2. **Secure the End**: Remove the braid from the disk and secure the ends with a temporary knot or clip.

3. Kongoh Gumi with Beads (Adding Beads to Basic Braid)

Step 1: Prepare Your Materials

1. **Thread Setup**: Cut four strands of thread, each about 1 meter (3 feet) long.
2. **Load Bobbins**: Thread each strand through a bobbin. Optionally, pre-string beads onto each thread before securing them on the kumihimo disk.

Step 2: Set Up the Kumihimo Disk

1. **Arrange Threads**: Place the threads into the slots of the kumihimo disk, alternating between threads with and without beads.
2. **Positioning**: Place the disk flat on your workspace with the dot at the top.

Step 3: Braiding Process

1. **Start Braiding**: Begin the braiding process as described in Technique 1, moving threads into empty slots.
2. **Add Beads**: When a beaded thread comes up in the rotation, slide a bead down to the braid. Push it up snugly

against the previous braid loop to secure it in place.
3. **Continue Braiding**: Alternate between moving threads and adding beads as you braid, maintaining even tension throughout.

Step 4: Finishing

1. **Complete the Braid**: Continue braiding until the desired length is achieved, ensuring beads are evenly distributed along the length of the braid.
2. **Secure the End**: Remove the braid from the disk and secure the ends with a knot or clasp, depending on your intended use.

INTERMEDIATE TECHNIQUES

Mastering intermediate kumihimo techniques requires building upon basic skills and adding complexity to achieve more intricate patterns and designs. Here are step-by-step instructions for three intermediate kumihimo techniques using a round disk:

Materials Needed:

- Kumihimo disk (round)
- Scissors
- Tama (bobbins) with thread (different colors for contrast)
- Optional: Beads or charms for embellishment

1. **Kara Gumi Hira(Flat Braid)**

Step 1: Prepare Your Materials

1. **Thread Setup**: Cut eight strands of thread, each approximately 1 meter (3 feet) long. Arrange them in pairs of complementary colors for a visually appealing design.
2. **Load Bobbins**: Thread each strand through a bobbin and secure them on the kumihimo disk.

Step 2: Set Up the Kumihimo Disk

1. **Arrange Threads**: Insert the threads into the slots of the kumihimo disk, positioning them so that each pair of opposite slots has threads of the same color.
2. **Positioning**: Place the disk flat on your workspace with the dot at the top.

Step 3: Braiding Process

1. **Start Braiding**: Begin by taking the bottom-right thread and move it to the top-right slot.
2. **Turn the Disk**: Rotate the disk so the bottom-left thread is now at the top-left slot.
3. **Continue Braiding**: Alternate between moving the bottom threads to the top slots in a diagonal pattern (right to left, then left to right). Maintain even tension throughout the process.
4. **Adjustments**: As you braid, adjust the tension and positioning of threads to ensure a flat braid formation.

Step 4: Finishing

1. **Repeat Braiding**: Continue braiding until the desired length is achieved.
2. **Secure the End**: Remove the braid from the disk and secure the ends with a temporary knot or clip.

2. Ayatake Gumi (Braided Diamond Pattern)

Step 1: Prepare Your Materials

1. **Thread Setup**: Cut twelve strands of thread, each approximately 1 meter (3 feet) long. Choose three colors to create a contrasting diamond pattern.
2. **Load Bobbins**: Thread each strand through a bobbin and secure them on the kumihimo disk.

Step 2: Set Up the Kumihimo Disk

1. **Arrange Threads**: Insert the threads into the slots of the kumihimo disk, alternating colors to create a pattern of three strands per slot.
2. **Positioning**: Place the disk flat on your workspace with the dot at the top.

Step 3: Braiding Process

1. **Start Braiding**: Begin by moving the bottom-right thread to the top-left slot, forming the first diagonal of the diamond pattern.
2. **Rotate and Braid**: Rotate the disk and continue moving threads in a diagonal pattern, alternating directions to create the diamond shapes. Keep track of the pattern sequence to maintain consistency.
3. **Adjust Tension**: As you braid, adjust the tension to ensure the diamond shapes are well-defined and evenly spaced.

Step 4: Finishing

1. **Complete the Braid**: Continue braiding until the desired length is achieved, ensuring the diamond pattern is consistent throughout.
2. **Secure the End**: Remove the braid from the disk and secure the ends with a knot or clasp suitable for your intended use.

3. Beaded Kumihimo with Spiral Pattern

Step 1: Prepare Your Materials

1. **Thread Setup**: Cut eight strands of thread, each approximately 1 meter (3 feet) long. Pre-string beads onto each strand in a pattern or randomly for a varied design.
2. **Load Bobbins**: Thread each strand through a bobbin and secure them on the kumihimo disk.

Step 2: Set Up the Kumihimo Disk

1. **Arrange Threads**: Insert the threads into the slots of the kumihimo disk, ensuring beads are positioned as desired for the spiral pattern.
2. **Positioning**: Place the disk flat on your workspace with the dot at the top.

Step 3: Braiding Process

1. **Start Braiding**: Begin braiding as in the basic round braid technique, moving threads into empty slots and rotating the disk after each move.
2. **Add Beads**: As you braid, slide beads down the threads into the forming braid. Place them snugly against the previous bead to create a spiral effect.

3. **Continue Braiding**: Alternate between moving threads and adding beads, maintaining even tension to keep the spiral pattern consistent.

Step 4: Finishing

1. **Complete the Braid**: Continue braiding until the desired length is achieved, ensuring beads are evenly distributed and the spiral pattern is visible.
2. **Secure the End**: Remove the braid from the disk and secure the ends with a knot or clasp suitable for your intended use.

By following these step-by-step instructions and tips, you can expand your kumihimo skills with intermediate techniques and create intricate, beautiful braids for various applications.

ADVANCED TECHNIQUES

Mastering advanced kumihimo techniques requires a combination of patience, precision, and creativity. Here are step-by-step instructions for two advanced kumihimo techniques, along with the materials needed for each:

Materials Needed:

- Kumihimo disk (round or square, depending on the technique)
- Scissors
- Tama (bobbins) with thread (different colors for contrast)
- Optional: Beads or charms for embellishment
- Weighted bobbins or clips to maintain tension
- Measuring tape or ruler

1. Kikkō Gumi (Hexagonal Braid)

Step 1: Prepare Your Materials

1. **Thread Setup**: Cut sixteen strands of thread, each approximately 1.5 meters (5 feet) long. Use two or more colors to create a visually appealing hexagonal pattern.
2. **Load Bobbins**: Thread each strand through a bobbin and secure them on the kumihimo disk.

Step 2: Set Up the Kumihimo Disk

1. **Arrange Threads**: Insert the threads into the slots of the kumihimo disk in pairs, alternating colors to form a hexagonal pattern.

2. **Positioning**: Place the disk flat on your workspace with the dot at the top.

Step 3: Braiding Process

1. **Start Braiding**: Position the disk so that there are eight pairs of threads, each occupying a slot. Ensure that the threads are arranged symmetrically around the disk.
2. **Initial Moves**: Move the top-right pair of threads to the bottom-right slot, and the bottom-left pair to the top-left slot.
3. **Rotate and Braid**: Rotate the disk 45 degrees clockwise and repeat the process. Move the pairs of threads in a similar manner, maintaining the hexagonal pattern.
4. **Maintain Tension**: Ensure even tension on the threads as you braid to keep the pattern consistent and the braid tight.

Step 4: Finishing

1. **Complete the Braid**: Continue braiding until the desired length is

achieved, ensuring the hexagonal pattern is consistent throughout.
2. **Secure the End**: Remove the braid from the disk and secure the ends with a knot or clasp suitable for your intended use.

2. **16-Strand Edo Yatsu Gumi with Beads (Advanced Square Braid with Beads)**

Step 1: Prepare Your Materials

1. **Thread Setup**: Cut sixteen strands of thread, each approximately 1 meter (3 feet) long. Pre-string beads onto

each strand in a pattern or randomly for a varied design.
2. **Load Bobbins**: Thread each strand through a bobbin and secure them on the kumihimo disk.

Step 2: Set Up the Kumihimo Disk

1. **Arrange Threads**: Insert the threads into the slots of the kumihimo disk in a symmetrical pattern, ensuring that the beads are positioned as desired for the square braid.
2. **Positioning**: Place the disk flat on your workspace with the dot at the top.

Step 3: Braiding Process

1. **Start Braiding**: Begin by taking the bottom-right thread pair and move it to the top-left slot.
2. **Rotate and Braid**: Rotate the disk and continue moving thread pairs in a diagonal pattern, alternating directions to create the square shapes.
3. **Add Beads**: As you braid, slide beads down the threads into the forming braid. Place them snugly against the previous bead to create a uniform effect.

4. **Adjust Tension**: Ensure even tension throughout the braiding process to keep the pattern consistent and the beads evenly spaced.

Step 4: Finishing

1. **Complete the Braid**: Continue braiding until the desired length is achieved, ensuring beads are evenly distributed and the square pattern is visible.
2. **Secure the End**: Remove the braid from the disk and secure the ends with a knot or clasp suitable for your intended use.

By following these step-by-step instructions and tips, you can expand your kumihimo skills with advanced techniques and create intricate, beautiful braids for various applications.

Troubleshooting and solutions

Kumihimo braiding, while rewarding, can present challenges that require troubleshooting. Here are common issues and solutions to help you achieve flawless braids:

1. Uneven Tension

Problem: Threads have inconsistent tension, leading to a lumpy or uneven braid.

Solution:

- **Check Bobbin Weights**: Ensure all bobbins have equal weights to maintain uniform tension.
- **Adjust Hand Tension**: Consistently apply the same tension when moving threads.
- **Practice**: Regular practice helps develop a feel for maintaining even tension.

2. Thread Slippage

Problem: Threads slip out of their slots, disrupting the pattern.

Solution:

- **Use Grippy Bobbins**: Ensure your bobbins grip the threads well.
- **Secure Threads**: Use a clip or knot to secure threads before starting the braid.

- **Check Disk Slots**: Make sure the slots on your kumihimo disk are not too wide for your threads.

3. Tangled Threads

Problem: Threads become tangled, making braiding difficult.

Solution:

- **Organize Bobbins**: Keep bobbins untangled and organized.
- **Use Bobbin Clips**: Secure the ends of threads with bobbin clips to prevent tangling.
- **Work Slowly**: Move threads deliberately and avoid rushing.

4. Misaligned Patterns

Problem: The braid pattern is not forming correctly.

Solution:

- **Double-Check Setup**: Ensure threads are correctly positioned before starting.
- **Follow Instructions**: Carefully follow the step-by-step braiding process.

- **Track Progress**: Mark the starting point on the disk to track your progress and catch mistakes early.

5. Fraying Threads

Problem: Threads fray or break during braiding.

Solution:

- **Use Quality Threads**: Invest in high-quality, durable threads suitable for kumihimo.
- **Handle with Care**: Avoid excessive pulling or tension that could cause fraying.
- **Seal Ends**: Use a fabric glue or clear nail polish to seal thread ends and prevent fraying.

6. Loose Beads

Problem: Beads are not staying in place within the braid.

Solution:

- **Secure Beads**: Push each bead snugly against the braid as you incorporate it.

- **Use Smaller Beads**: Ensure bead holes are not too large for the thread.
- **Add Beads Strategically**: Incorporate beads at regular intervals to maintain pattern consistency.

7. Incorrect Length

Problem: The braid is either too short or too long.

Solution:

- **Measure Twice**: Measure the desired length before starting and periodically check during braiding.
- **Account for Stretch**: Some threads stretch slightly during braiding; consider this when measuring.

8. Difficulty with Complex Patterns

Problem: Advanced patterns are challenging to execute accurately.

Solution:

- **Simplify Steps**: Break down complex patterns into simpler, manageable steps.

- **Use a Pattern Guide**: Follow a visual guide or diagram for intricate patterns.
- **Practice Basic Techniques**: Ensure proficiency in basic techniques before attempting advanced patterns.

9. Disk Wear and Tear

Problem: The kumihimo disk wears out or loses its shape.

Solution:

- **Choose Quality Disks**: Invest in durable disks that withstand frequent use.
- **Rotate Use**: If you have multiple disks, rotate their use to prevent excessive wear on one disk.
- **Replace When Necessary**: Replace worn-out disks to maintain braiding precision.

10. Thread Tension Changes During Braiding

Problem: Tension changes as the braid progresses, causing inconsistencies.

Solution:

- **Re-adjust Bobbins Regularly**: Periodically check and adjust the tension of the bobbins.
- **Use a Weight**: Attach a small weight to the end of the braid to maintain consistent downward tension.
- **Mindful Handling**: Be mindful of your grip and tension throughout the braiding process.

By addressing these common issues with the suggested solutions, you can improve your kumihimo braiding technique and create beautiful, consistent braids.

Chapter 3

BEGINNERS PROJECT

Creating beginner kumihimo projects helps build foundational skills while producing attractive and useful items. Here are eight beginner kumihimo projects, each with step-by-step instructions and a list of materials needed.

Project 1: Basic Round Braid Bracelet

Materials Needed:

- Kumihimo disk (round)
- 8 strands of embroidery floss or satin cord (1 meter each)
- Scissors
- Tape or clip

Steps:

1. **Cut Threads**: Cut 8 strands of floss or cord, each about 1 meter long.
2. **Arrange Threads**: Tie the ends together in an overhand knot and place it through the center hole of the kumihimo disk. Arrange the threads in the slots around the disk (two strands per quadrant).
3. **Start Braiding**: Take the bottom right thread and move it to the top right slot. Then take the top left thread and move it to the bottom left slot.
4. **Rotate Disk**: Rotate the disk 90 degrees clockwise and repeat the process.
5. **Continue Braiding**: Repeat until the desired bracelet length is achieved.
6. **Finish**: Tie the end with an overhand knot and trim any excess thread.

Project 2: Beaded Kumihimo Bracelet

Materials Needed:

- Kumihimo disk (round)
- 8 strands of beading thread (1 meter each)
- Small beads
- Scissors
- Tape or clip

Steps:

1. **Cut Threads**: Cut 8 strands of beading thread, each about 1 meter long.
2. **String Beads**: Thread beads onto each strand, securing them in place.

3. **Arrange Threads**: Tie the ends together in an overhand knot and place it through the center hole of the kumihimo disk. Arrange the threads in the slots around the disk.
4. **Start Braiding**: Begin the braiding process as in Project 1, adding a bead into each thread movement.
5. **Continue Braiding**: Repeat until the desired length is achieved.
6. **Finish**: Tie the end with an overhand knot and trim any excess thread.

Project 3: Keychain

Materials Needed:

- Kumihimo disk (round)
- 8 strands of embroidery floss (1 meter each)
- Keyring
- Scissors

Steps:

1. **Cut Threads**: Cut 8 strands of floss, each about 1 meter long.
2. **Attach to Keyring**: Tie the ends together and loop them through the keyring, securing them in place.
3. **Arrange Threads**: Place the threads through the center hole of the kumihimo disk and arrange them in the slots.
4. **Start Braiding**: Follow the basic round braid technique.
5. **Continue Braiding**: Braid until the desired length is achieved.
6. **Finish**: Tie the end with an overhand knot and trim any excess thread.

Project 4: Simple Necklace

Materials Needed:

- Kumihimo disk (round)
- 8 strands of satin cord (1.5 meters each)
- Clasp
- Scissors

Steps:

1. **Cut Threads**: Cut 8 strands of satin cord, each about 1.5 meters long.
2. **Arrange Threads**: Tie the ends together and place through the center hole of the kumihimo disk.

3. **Start Braiding**: Use the basic round braid technique.
4. **Continue Braiding**: Braid until the desired length is achieved.
5. **Attach Clasp**: Secure the ends with knots and attach the clasp.
6. **Finish**: Trim any excess thread.

Project 5: Phone Charm

Materials Needed:

- Kumihimo disk (round)
- 8 strands of embroidery floss (1 meter each)
- Charm

- Phone strap loop
- Scissors

Steps:

1. **Cut Threads**: Cut 8 strands of floss, each about 1 meter long.
2. **Attach Charm**: Tie the threads together with the charm at the end.
3. **Arrange Threads**: Place the threads through the center hole of the kumihimo disk.
4. **Start Braiding**: Use the basic round braid technique.
5. **Continue Braiding**: Braid until the desired length is achieved.
6. **Attach Phone Loop**: Secure the end with a knot and attach the phone strap loop.
7. **Finish**: Trim any excess thread.

Project 6: Anklet

Materials Needed:

- Kumihimo disk (round)
- 8 strands of cotton thread (1 meter each)
- Beads (optional)
- Clasp
- Scissors

Steps:

1. **Cut Threads**: Cut 8 strands of cotton thread, each about 1 meter long.

2. **String Beads**: (Optional) Thread beads onto each strand.
3. **Arrange Threads**: Tie the ends together and place through the center hole of the kumihimo disk.
4. **Start Braiding**: Use the basic round braid technique.
5. **Continue Braiding**: Braid until the desired length is achieved.
6. **Attach Clasp**: Secure the ends with knots and attach the clasp.
7. **Finish**: Trim any excess thread.

Project 7: Headband

Materials Needed:

- Kumihimo disk (round)
- 12 strands of satin cord (1.5 meters each)
- Elastic band
- Scissors

Steps:

1. **Cut Threads**: Cut 12 strands of satin cord, each about 1.5 meters long.
2. **Arrange Threads**: Tie the ends together and place through the center hole of the kumihimo disk. Arrange the threads in the slots.
3. **Start Braiding**: Use a more complex braid technique (e.g., 12-strand round braid).
4. **Continue Braiding**: Braid until the desired length is achieved.
5. **Attach Elastic**: Secure the ends with knots and attach an elastic band to make the headband stretchable.
6. **Finish**: Trim any excess thread.

Project 8: Lanyard

Materials Needed:

- Kumihimo disk (round)
- 16 strands of paracord (2 meters each)
- Lanyard clip
- Scissors

Steps:

1. **Cut Threads**: Cut 16 strands of paracord, each about 2 meters long.
2. **Attach to Clip**: Tie the ends together and loop them through the lanyard clip.

3. **Arrange Threads**: Place the threads through the center hole of the kumihimo disk.
4. **Start Braiding**: Use the 16-strand round braid technique.
5. **Continue Braiding**: Braid until the desired length is achieved.
6. **Finish**: Secure the end with a knot and trim any excess cord.

By following these step-by-step instructions and gathering the necessary materials, you can create a variety of beginner kumihimo projects and build a strong foundation for more advanced braiding techniques.

INTERMEDIATE PROJECTS

Building on basic skills, intermediate kumihimo projects introduce more complexity and creativity. Here are five intermediate kumihimo projects with step-by-step instructions and materials needed.

Project 1: Spiral Beaded Kumihimo Bracelet

Materials Needed:

- Kumihimo disk (round)
- 8 strands of beading thread (1 meter each)
- Small beads
- Clasp
- Scissors
- Bobbins

Steps:

1. **Cut Threads**: Cut 8 strands of beading thread, each about 1 meter long.
2. **String Beads**: Thread beads onto each strand, securing them in place.
3. **Arrange Threads**: Tie the ends together in an overhand knot and place it through the center hole of the kumihimo disk. Arrange the threads in the slots around the disk.
4. **Start Braiding**: Begin the braiding process as in the basic round braid technique, adding a bead into each thread movement.
5. **Continue Braiding**: Repeat until the desired bracelet length is achieved.
6. **Attach Clasp**: Secure the ends with knots and attach the clasp.
7. **Finish**: Trim any excess thread.

Project 2: Flat Braided Necklace with Charms

Materials Needed:

- Kumihimo disk (round)

- 8 strands of satin cord (1.5 meters each)
- Charms
- Clasp
- Scissors
- Bobbins

Steps:

1. **Cut Threads**: Cut 8 strands of satin cord, each about 1.5 meters long.
2. **Attach Charms**: Thread charms onto the satin cords, spacing them evenly.
3. **Arrange Threads**: Tie the ends together in an overhand knot and place it through the center hole of the kumihimo disk.
4. **Start Braiding**: Use the flat braid technique (Hira Kara Gumi). Begin by moving the bottom-right thread to the top-right slot, then the bottom-left thread to the top-left slot.
5. **Rotate Disk**: Rotate the disk 90 degrees clockwise and repeat the process.
6. **Continue Braiding**: Braid until the desired length is achieved, ensuring charms are evenly incorporated.
7. **Attach Clasp**: Secure the ends with knots and attach the clasp.
8. **Finish**: Trim any excess thread.

Project 3: Two-Color Spiral Bracelet

Materials Needed:

- Kumihimo disk (round)
- 4 strands of one color thread (1 meter each)
- 4 strands of another color thread (1 meter each)
- Clasp
- Scissors
- Bobbins

Steps:

1. **Cut Threads**: Cut 4 strands of one color and 4 strands of another color, each about 1 meter long.
2. **Arrange Threads**: Tie the ends together in an overhand knot and place it through the center hole of the kumihimo disk. Arrange the threads in the slots so that colors alternate.
3. **Start Braiding**: Use the basic round braid technique, moving the bottom-right thread to the top-right slot and the top-left thread to the bottom-left slot.
4. **Rotate Disk**: Rotate the disk 90 degrees clockwise and repeat the process.
5. **Continue Braiding**: Braid until the desired length is achieved, creating a spiral pattern with the two colors.
6. **Attach Clasp**: Secure the ends with knots and attach the clasp.
7. **Finish**: Trim any excess thread.

Project 4: Beaded Kumihimo Lanyard

Materials Needed:

- Kumihimo disk (round)
- 8 strands of beading thread (2 meters each)
- Small beads
- Lanyard clip
- Scissors
- Bobbins

Steps:

1. **Cut Threads**: Cut 8 strands of beading thread, each about 2 meters long.
2. **String Beads**: Thread beads onto each strand, securing them in place.
3. **Attach to Clip**: Tie the ends together and loop them through the lanyard clip, securing them in place.
4. **Arrange Threads**: Place the threads through the center hole of the kumihimo disk.
5. **Start Braiding**: Begin the braiding process as in the basic round braid technique, adding a bead into each thread movement.
6. **Continue Braiding**: Braid until the desired lanyard length is achieved.
7. **Finish**: Secure the end with a knot and trim any excess thread.

Project 5: Mixed Media Kumihimo Bracelet

Materials Needed:

- Kumihimo disk (round)
- 8 strands of various cords and threads (e.g., satin cord, leather cord, embroidery floss) (1 meter each)
- Beads and charms (optional)
- Clasp
- Scissors
- Bobbins

Steps:

1. **Cut Threads**: Cut 8 strands of various cords and threads, each about 1 meter long.
2. **Arrange Threads**: Tie the ends together in an overhand knot and place it through the center hole of the kumihimo disk.
3. **Start Braiding**: Use the basic round braid technique, incorporating different textures and thicknesses of threads and cords.
4. **Add Beads and Charms**: (Optional) Thread beads and charms onto the cords and threads as you braid.
5. **Continue Braiding**: Braid until the desired bracelet length is achieved.
6. **Attach Clasp**: Secure the ends with knots and attach the clasp.
7. **Finish**: Trim any excess thread.

By following these step-by-step instructions and gathering the necessary materials, you can create a variety of intermediate kumihimo projects that showcase your developing skills and creativity.

ADVANCED PROJECTS

Advanced kumihimo projects involve more complex patterns and techniques, often incorporating multiple strands, beads, or intricate designs. Here are three advanced kumihimo projects with step-by-step instructions and materials needed.

Project 1: 16-Strand Kongo Gumi Beaded Necklace

Materials Needed:

- Kumihimo disk (round)

- 16 strands of beading thread (1.5 meters each)
- Small beads (size 6/0 or 8/0)
- Clasp
- Scissors
- Bobbins

Steps:

1. **Cut Threads**: Cut 16 strands of beading thread, each about 1.5 meters long.
2. **String Beads**: Thread beads onto each strand. You'll need approximately 100 beads per strand, depending on the desired length.
3. **Arrange Threads**: Tie the ends together in an overhand knot and place it through the center hole of the kumihimo disk. Arrange the threads in pairs in the slots around the disk.
4. **Start Braiding**: Use the 16-strand Kongo Gumi technique. Move the top-left thread of one pair to the bottom-left slot and the bottom-right thread of another pair to the top-right slot. Rotate the disk 45 degrees counterclockwise and repeat.
5. **Add Beads**: Incorporate beads into the braid by sliding a bead down each

thread before moving it to the new slot.
6. **Continue Braiding**: Braid until the desired necklace length is achieved, ensuring beads are evenly spaced and the braid is tight.
7. **Attach Clasp**: Secure the ends with knots and attach the clasp using jewelry findings.
8. **Finish**: Trim any excess thread.

Project 2: Flat Braid Bracelet with Beads (Hira Kara Gumi)

Materials Needed:

- Kumihimo disk (square)

- 10 strands of satin cord or embroidery floss (1 meter each)
- Small beads
- Clasp
- Scissors
- Bobbins

Steps:

1. **Cut Threads**: Cut 10 strands of satin cord or embroidery floss, each about 1 meter long.
2. **String Beads**: Thread beads onto each strand, securing them in place.
3. **Arrange Threads**: Tie the ends together in an overhand knot and place it through the center hole of the kumihimo disk. Arrange the threads in the slots on the square disk.
4. **Start Braiding**: Use the Hira Kara Gumi technique. Move the bottom-center thread to the top-center slot and the top-center thread to the bottom-center slot. Then, move the right-center thread to the left-center slot and the left-center thread to the right-center slot. Rotate the disk 90 degrees clockwise and repeat.
5. **Add Beads**: Slide beads down the threads as you braid, incorporating them into the flat braid.

6. **Continue Braiding**: Braid until the desired bracelet length is achieved.
7. **Attach Clasp**: Secure the ends with knots and attach the clasp.
8. **Finish**: Trim any excess thread.

Project 3: Spiral Kumihimo Rope with Beads (Edo Yatsu Gumi)

Materials Needed:

- Kumihimo disk (round)
- 8 strands of beading thread (1.5 meters each)
- Small beads (size 6/0 or 8/0)

- Clasp
- Scissors
- Bobbins

Steps:

1. **Cut Threads**: Cut 8 strands of beading thread, each about 1.5 meters long.
2. **String Beads**: Thread beads onto each strand, securing them in place. You'll need approximately 80 beads per strand.
3. **Arrange Threads**: Tie the ends together in an overhand knot and place it through the center hole of the kumihimo disk. Arrange the threads in the slots around the disk in pairs.
4. **Start Braiding**: Use the Edo Yatsu Gumi technique. Move the top-right thread to the bottom-right slot and the bottom-left thread to the top-left slot. Rotate the disk 90 degrees clockwise and repeat.
5. **Add Beads**: Slide beads down the threads and incorporate them into the braid.
6. **Continue Braiding**: Braid until the desired rope length is achieved.
7. **Attach Clasp**: Secure the ends with knots and attach the clasp.
8. **Finish**: Trim any excess thread.

By following these step-by-step instructions and gathering the necessary materials, you can create a variety of advanced kumihimo projects that showcase your skills and creativity.

TIPS FOR SUCCESS

Achieving beautiful and professional kumihimo braids requires patience, practice, and attention to detail. Here are some tips to ensure success in your kumihimo projects:

1. Choose the Right Materials

- **Quality Threads and Cords**: Invest in high-quality threads and cords. Satin cords, silk threads, and embroidery floss work well for various projects.
- **Appropriate Beads**: Select beads with holes large enough to accommodate your threads but not so large that they slide around. Beads like seed beads, pearls, and gemstone beads are popular choices.

2. Use the Right Tools

- **Kumihimo Disk**: Use a durable and well-cut kumihimo disk. Foam disks

are popular for their flexibility and ease of use.
- **Bobbins**: Bobbins help keep your threads organized and prevent tangling. They are especially useful for longer threads.
- **Clamps and Weights**: Use a kumihimo weight or a small binder clip with a weight to maintain even tension and keep your work steady.

3. Maintain Consistent Tension

- **Even Tension**: Consistent tension is key to creating uniform braids. Ensure that all strands are pulled with the same force.
- **Check Regularly**: Periodically check your tension and adjust as needed to avoid lumpy or uneven braids.

4. Keep an Organized Workspace

- **Tidy Workspace**: A clean and organized workspace helps you avoid mistakes and makes the braiding process smoother.
- **Thread Management**: Use bobbins to manage your threads and prevent tangling. Keep them neatly wound and clipped.

5. Follow Patterns Carefully

- **Step-by-Step Instructions**: Follow instructions carefully, especially for complex patterns. Missing a step can alter the design.
- **Visual Guides**: Use visual guides, charts, or diagrams to help keep track of your pattern. Marking your starting point on the disk can help track your progress.

6. Practice Basic Techniques

- **Master Basics**: Before tackling advanced projects, ensure you are comfortable with basic braiding techniques. Mastering the basics lays a strong foundation for more complex designs.
- **Simple Projects**: Start with simple projects to build your skills and confidence.

7. Experiment and Be Creative

- **Color Combinations**: Experiment with different color combinations and textures to create unique designs.
- **Mix Materials**: Don't be afraid to mix different types of threads, cords, and beads for interesting effects.

8. Use Quality Findings

- **Secure Endings**: Use strong and appropriate findings, such as clasps and end caps, to ensure your braid stays intact.
- **Finish Neatly**: Trim any excess threads neatly and use a dab of glue to secure knots if necessary.

9. Stay Patient and Persistent

- **Take Your Time**: Advanced kumihimo braiding takes time and precision. Don't rush the process.
- **Practice Regularly**: Regular practice helps improve your skills and develop a feel for maintaining even tension and following patterns accurately.

10. Learn from Mistakes

- **Identify Issues**: If something doesn't look right, identify the issue early. Unbraid a few steps if needed to correct mistakes.
- **Keep Trying**: Don't get discouraged by mistakes. They are vital to your growth as a learner and contribute to your progress.

11. Seek Inspiration and Tutorials

- **Online Resources**: Utilize online tutorials, videos, and forums for inspiration and learning new techniques.
- **Books and Guides**: Invest in good books and guides on kumihimo braiding for reference and new project ideas.

12. Keep a Kumihimo Journal

- **Document Projects**: Keep a journal of your projects, noting the patterns, materials used, and any adjustments made.
- **Track Progress**: Documenting your work helps track your progress and serves as a valuable reference for future projects.

By following these tips, you can enhance your kumihimo braiding skills and create beautiful, professional-looking braids. Remember, practice and patience are key to mastering the art of kumihimo.

Conclusion

Kumihimo is a captivating and versatile braiding technique with deep historical roots and endless creative possibilities. Whether you're a beginner starting with simple round braids or an advanced braider experimenting with intricate patterns and beadwork, kumihimo offers a fulfilling artistic journey.

By choosing the right materials, maintaining consistent tension, keeping an organized workspace, and practicing regularly, you can create beautiful and professional-looking kumihimo projects. Don't hesitate to experiment with colors, textures, and different types of threads and beads to make your designs unique.

Remember, patience and persistence are key to mastering kumihimo. Mistakes are part of the learning process, and each project you complete will enhance your skills and creativity. Keep seeking inspiration, learning new techniques, and documenting your progress to continually improve and enjoy the art of kumihimo braiding.